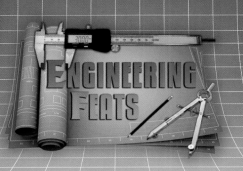

Orion Spacecraft

Earle Rice Jr.

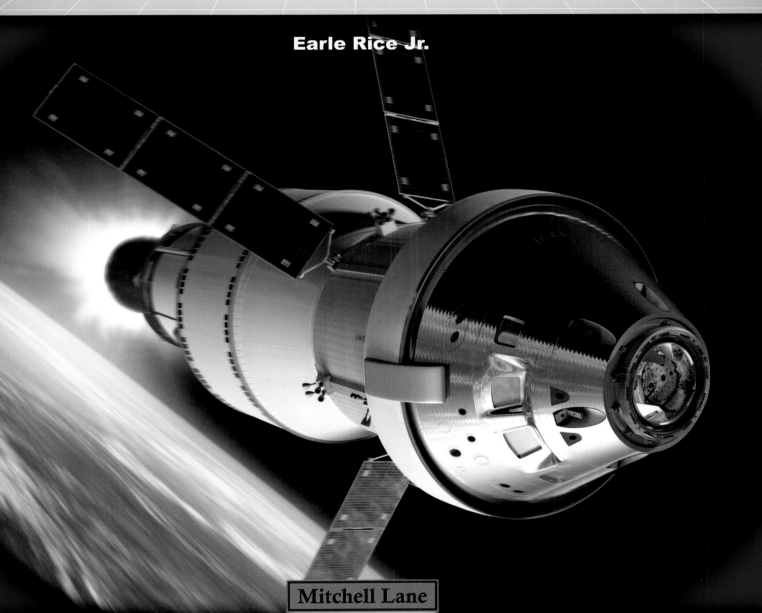

Mitchell Lane
PUBLISHERS

2001 SW 31st Avenue
Hallandale, FL 33009
www.mitchelllane.com

Mitchell Lane
PUBLISHERS

Printing   1   2   3   4   5   6   7   8

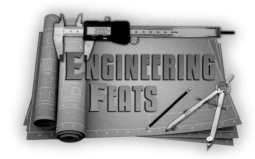

Designer: Sharon Beck
Editor: Jim Whiting

Library of Congress Cataloging-in-Publication Data
Names: Rice, Earle, Jr., 1928- author.
Title: The Orion Spacecraft / by Earle Rice Jr.
Description: Hallandale, FL : Mitchell Lane Publishers, [2018] | Series: Engineering feats | Includes
    bibliographical references and index. | Audience: Grades 4 to 6.
Identifiers: LCCN 2017046709 | ISBN 9781680201680 (library bound)
Subjects: LCSH: Orion (Spacecraft)—Juvenile literature. | Manned space flight—Juvenile literature.
    | Space vehicles—United States—Juvenile literature.
Classification: LCC TL789.8.U6 O757 2018 | DDC 629.45—dc23
LC record available at https://lccn.loc.gov/2017046709

eBook ISBN: 9-781-68020-169-7

PHOTO CREDITS: Design elements—RED_SPY/Getty Images, Ifness/Getty Images, Madmaxer/Getty Images, chictype/Getty Images, Thissatan/Getty Images, Nongkran_ch/Getty Images. Back cover photos (left to right)—NASA/JPL, Imagine China/Newscom, Henryk Sadura/Getty Images, NASA, Rehman/cc by-sa 2.0, U.S. Navy/Mass Communication Specialist Seaman Casey Hopkins/Public domain. Cover, pp. 1, 8, 9, 10, 11, 13 (inset), 14, 15, 19, 20, 21, 23, 25, 26, 28, 29, 30, 33, 34, 36, 37—NASA; p. 5—NASA/Sandra Joseph and Kevin O'Connell, (inset)—NASA/Kim Shiflett; pp. 6-7 (background) and p. 7 (inset)—U.S. Navy Photo/Mass Communication Specialist 1st Class Charles White/Public domain; p. 6 (inset)—blogs.nasa.gov & NASA; p. 8 (inset)—NASA/Harrison Schmitt; p. 13—Adrian Mann/ Stocktrek Images/Getty Images; p. 16 (inset)—Edgar D. Mitchell/NASA; p. 17—NASA/Crew of STS-132; p. 19 (inset)—Lockheed Martin Corporation/NASA; p. 27—Lockheed Martin/NASA; p. 28—NASA/Dimitri Gerondidakis; p. 30—NASA/Rad Sinyak; p. 33—U.S. Military/ Department of Defense/Public domain; p. 37—Sasha Congiu/NASA Langley Research Center; p. 38—NASA, Lockheed Martin and Orbital ATK; p. 39—NASA Engineering & Safety Center (NESC), (inset)—United Launch Alliance/NASA; p. 48— NASA/Bill Stafford. All photos courtesy of NASA are in the public domain.

CONTENTS

Words in **bold** throughout can be found in the Glossary.

Back to the Future

On December 5, 2014, at 7:05 on a clear winter morning, the National Aeronautics and Space Administration (NASA) took the first step on its planned journey to the far distant planet of Mars. The distance between Earth and the Red Planet, as Mars is often called, varies. It depends on where they are in their two orbits on any given day, month, or year. On average, they are 140 million miles (225 million kilometers)[1] apart. That's almost 60 times the distance from Earth to the moon! So just as a baby must crawl before it walks, NASA must take small steps before it attempts another "giant leap for mankind,"[2] as **astronaut** Neil Armstrong put it a half-century ago.

At Cape Canaveral Air Force Station's Launch Complex 37 in Florida, the cone-shaped Orion spacecraft blazed into the morning sky atop a Delta IV Heavy rocket. It was Orion's first uncrewed test flight, called Exploration Flight Test-1 (EFT-1). For the first time in more than 40 years, a spacecraft built for humans soared outside low-Earth orbit.

On this morning, during a 4.5-hour flight, Orion circled the Earth twice. It flew two times through the Van Allen belts, experiencing intense periods of radiation, while reaching an altitude of 3,600 miles (5,800 kilometers) above Earth. Attaining speeds of more than 20,000 mph (32000 k/hr), it withstood temperatures nearing 4,000 degrees

NASA's Orion spacecraft lifts off aboard a Delta IV Heavy rocket at Space Launch Complex 37 (shown in inset) at Cape Canaveral Air Force Station in Florida on an unpiloted, Earth-orbital test flight. During a two-orbit, four-and-a-half hour mission, engineers evaluated systems critical to crew safety—the launch abort system, the heat shield, and the parachute system.

Fahrenheit (2,200 degrees Celsius) as it reentered the Earth's atmosphere. After a highly successful flight, Orion splashed down in the Pacific Ocean, 600 miles (966 kilograms) south of San Diego.

A team aboard the USS *Anchorage* (LPD-23) stood by to track and recover Orion. The team stayed in constant contact with Johnson Space Center in Houston for real-time tracking information. Before leaving port in San Diego, Lieutenant Keith Tate, *Anchorage*'s operations officer, said,

Upon its return from a two-orbit, four-and-a-half hour test flight, the Orion crew module parachuted back to Earth and splashed down safely in the Pacific Ocean. A veteran team of personnel from NASA, the Navy, and prime contractor Lockheed Martin aboard the USS *Anchorage* retrieved it and returned it to the naval base at San Diego.

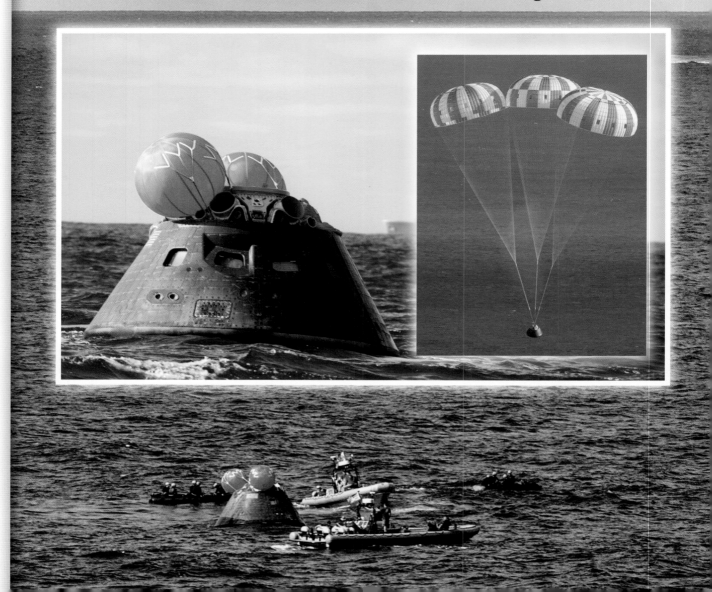

"All of us who have been here since the beginning are excited to see this day come. We're hoping for a safe, successful evolution. It's something historic and we're all proud to be a part of it."[3]

The team recovered Orion without a hitch and returned it to Naval Base San Diego. From there, it was transported by truck to Kennedy Space Center, just northwest of Cape Canaveral. After refurbishing, the crew **module** will be used to test Orion's launch abort system in 2019.

USS *Anchorage* (LPD 23)

Sailors aboard the USS *Anchorage* recover parachutes from the NASA's Orion crew module following a successful splashdown after Exploration Flight Test 1 (EFT-1), the first exploration flight of the spacecraft. It was the fifth test of the module at sea using a Navy well deck-recovery method.

At the outset of the first Apollo 17 Extravehicular Activity (EVA-1), astronaut Eugene A. Cernan checks out the Lunar Roving Vehicle (LRV) against a backdrop of deep-space blackness at a lunar landing site known as Taurus-Littrow.

Cernan in the Lunar Module after EVA-3

FAST FACT

On December 14, 1972, Apollo 17 became the last mission to land men on the moon. It was commanded by astronaut Eugene Cernan.

"Today's flight test of Orion is a huge step for NASA and a really critical part of our work to pioneer **deep space** on our journey to Mars," said NASA administrator Charles Bolden. "The teams did a tremendous job putting Orion through its paces in the real environment it will endure as we push the boundary of human exploration in the coming years."[4] NASA's immediate targeted boundary is the space between Earth and Mars.

Engineers designed EFT-1 to test capabilities needed for future missions to Mars, which are scheduled to begin in the 2030s. Testing Orion in space enabled them to gather critical data. They then evaluated the craft's performance and used their findings to improve its design. Systems tested during the flight included Orion's heat shield, avionics, computers, and parachutes. Ensuring that these and other systems function properly is vital to the safety of astronauts who will travel into deep space in Orion.

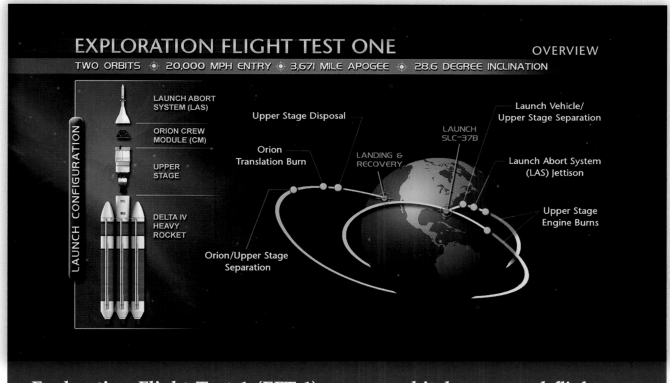

EXPLORATION FLIGHT TEST ONE   OVERVIEW

TWO ORBITS ◈ 20,000 MPH ENTRY ◈ 3,671 MILE APOGEE ◈ 28.6 DEGREE INCLINATION

LAUNCH CONFIGURATION

LAUNCH ABORT SYSTEM (LAS)

ORION CREW MODULE (CM)

UPPER STAGE

DELTA IV HEAVY ROCKET

Upper Stage Disposal

Orion Translation Burn

LANDING & RECOVERY

Orion/Upper Stage Separation

Launch Vehicle/ Upper Stage Separation

LAUNCH SLC-37B

Launch Abort System (LAS) Jettison

Upper Stage Engine Burns

Exploration Flight Test 1 (EFT-1) was an orbital, uncrewed flight conducted in 2014 to test minimum mission/flight requirements. It ran MPVC system-level tests and explored risk reduction opportunities. Three additional tests to provide more system-level testing and shakedown will consist of Ascent Abort 2 (AA-2), an abort test in a high dynamic pressure environment; Exploration Mission 1 (EM-1), an uncrewed BEO (Beyond Earth Orbit, a lunar flyby); and EM-2, a crewed BEO flight (including a 3-4 day lunar orbit).

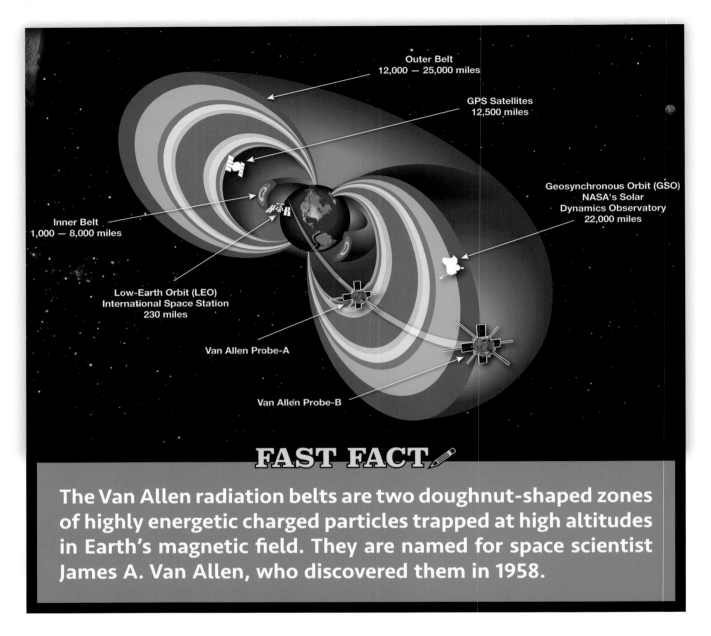

Outer Belt
12,000 — 25,000 miles

GPS Satellites
12,500 miles

Geosynchronous Orbit (GSO)
NASA's Solar
Dynamics Observatory
22,000 miles

Inner Belt
1,000 — 8,000 miles

Low-Earth Orbit (LEO)
International Space Station
230 miles

Van Allen Probe-A

Van Allen Probe-B

FAST FACT ✎

The Van Allen radiation belts are two doughnut-shaped zones of highly energetic charged particles trapped at high altitudes in Earth's magnetic field. They are named for space scientist James A. Van Allen, who discovered them in 1958.

"We really pushed Orion as much as we could to give us real data that we can use to improve Orion's design going forward," said Orion program manager Mark Geyer. "In the coming weeks and months we'll be taking a look at the invaluable information and applying lessons learned to the next Orion spacecraft already in production for the first mission atop the Space Launch System rocket."[5]

The next unmanned mission for Orion is scheduled for early 2019. It will use NASA's Space Launch System (SLS). The SLS is the most powerful rocket NASA has ever built. It is now under development at the agency's

Marshall Space Flight Center in Huntsville, Alabama. The 77-ton (70-metric ton) rocket will insert Orion in a distant **retrograde**—backward—orbit around the moon. Designated Exploration Mission 1 (EM-1), it will be the first flight to test the full **integration**—two or more systems functioning as one—of Orion and the SLS rocket.

The first manned flight—Exploration Mission 2 (EM-2)—will carry astronauts around the moon for between eight and 21 days. It was initially scheduled for 2021 but may slip to 2023 or later.

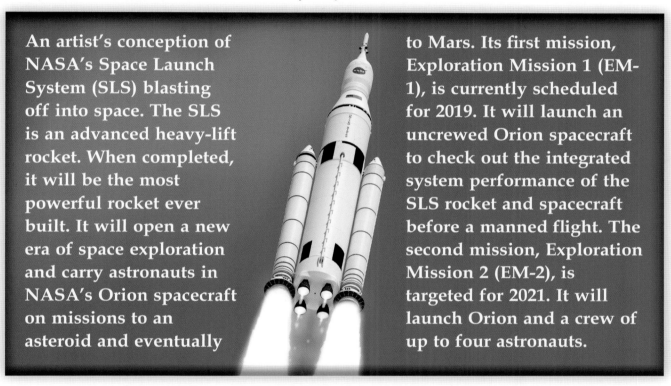

An artist's conception of NASA's Space Launch System (SLS) blasting off into space. The SLS is an advanced heavy-lift rocket. When completed, it will be the most powerful rocket ever built. It will open a new era of space exploration and carry astronauts in NASA's Orion spacecraft on missions to an asteroid and eventually to Mars. Its first mission, Exploration Mission 1 (EM-1), is currently scheduled for 2019. It will launch an uncrewed Orion spacecraft to check out the integrated system performance of the SLS rocket and spacecraft before a manned flight. The second mission, Exploration Mission 2 (EM-2), is targeted for 2021. It will launch Orion and a crew of up to four astronauts.

EFT-1 evoked a sense of **déjà vu**—the feeling of having previously experienced a present situation—among the Orion team members who recalled the Apollo program. And for good reason. Apollo veterans served on the recovery ship and in Mission Control in Houston. They enjoyed getting back together to do what they love to do. "We haven't had this feeling in a while, since the end of the shuttle program,"[6] said Mike Serafin, EFT-1's lead flight director. The feeling is likely to persist, since much of the Orion program is built on lessons learned during the Apollo and Space Shuttle programs.

2
New Life

"There's an obvious comparison to draw between the first Orion launch and the first unmanned flight of the Apollo spacecraft on Apollo 4 [in 1967]," said space historian Amy Teitel, "but there are more differences than similarities."[1] The Apollo command module (CM) carried astronauts to the moon in the 1960s. Though Orion strongly resembles the Apollo CM, it is crammed with the latest technological advances. Today's technology alone sets it apart from Apollo and yesteryear's state of the art. And there are numerous other differences.

Both modules are cone-shaped and use a large heat shield to protect crew members from intense reentry conditions. Orion is larger, however, and will carry four to six people, rather than Apollo's three. Also, Orion will need to carry more supplies than its predecessor. As with Apollo, a service module (SM) will be attached to Orion's command module. It will house a single large engine, batteries, and storage. In addition, a pair of **solar** arrays will help power Orion in space. Apollo did not have this technology.

Further, Orion uses advanced computers, electronics, life support, and propulsion systems. It features a much-improved heat shield, covered with a new material called **Avcoat**. Measuring 16.5 feet (5 meters) across, it is the largest heat shield ever built for a space vehicle. A new parachute system will ensure Orion's safe water landings.

Orion Command/Service Module (CSM) in Earth orbit draws additional power from its windmill-like solar array. The Skylab 4 Command/Service Module (inset) docks with Skylab, America's first space station. Skylab paved the way for the International Space Station (ISS).

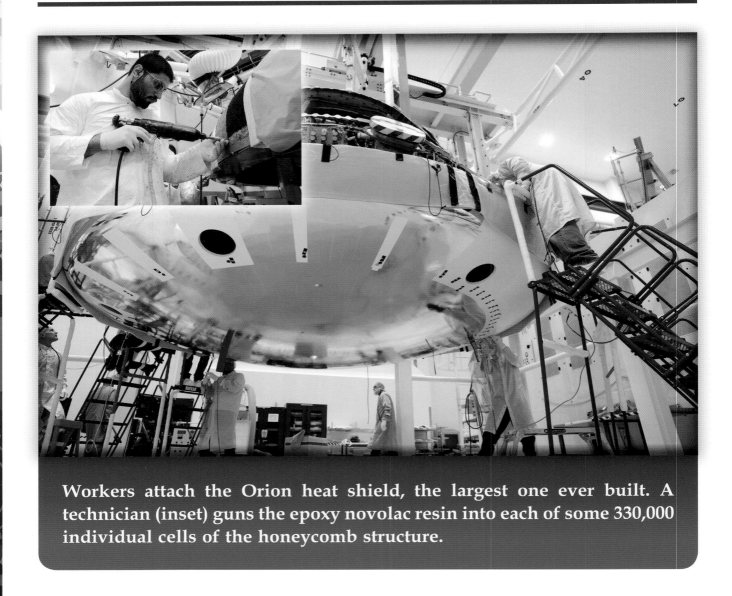

Workers attach the Orion heat shield, the largest one ever built. A technician (inset) guns the epoxy novolac resin into each of some 330,000 individual cells of the honeycomb structure.

"With Apollo 4," Teitel continued, "we knew we were going to the moon and it was clear this mission was putting us firmly back on that path after the major setback of the Apollo 1 fire. With Orion, we don't have a clear goal and a firm timeline for this new spacecraft."[2]

President John F. Kennedy established Apollo's clear mission during an address to Congress on May 25, 1961. He said, "I believe that this nation should commit itself to achieving the goal, before this decade is out, of landing a man on the moon and returning him safely to the earth. No single space project in this period will be more impressive to mankind, or more important for the long-range exploration of space."[3]

Grissom, White, and Chaffee

FAST FACT ✎

On January 27, 1967, a fire broke out in the Apollo 1 capsule. Command pilot Virgil "Gus" Grissom, senior pilot Edward White II, and pilot Roger Chaffee died in the blaze. They were scheduled to take Apollo 1 on its first crewed flight into low-Earth orbit.

Three weeks earlier, on May 5, astronaut Alan Shepard had blasted off in the Mercury spacecraft Freedom 7 to become the first American in space. Encouraged by Shepard's feat, President Kennedy wanted to move ahead faster with the program. He asked Congress to add $7 to $9 billion to the moon-landing program over the next five years. Critics doubted NASA's ability to achieve the task in such a short time frame. NASA paid them no mind.

On February 20 the following year, John Glenn Jr. became the first American to orbit the Earth in the Mercury spacecraft Friendship 7. Project Mercury (1958–1963) was America's first manned space program. Mercury astronauts flew longer and longer missions, collecting data for programs to follow. Project Gemini (1961–1966) astronauts flew low-Earth orbits between 1965 and 1966. They perfected spacecraft entry and reentry maneuvers and conducted tests on the effects of prolonged space travel on individuals. They gave the United States a leg up in its Cold War space race with the then-Soviet Union.

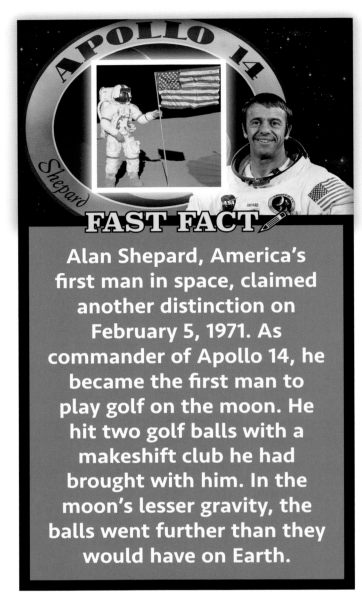

FAST FACT

Alan Shepard, America's first man in space, claimed another distinction on February 5, 1971. As commander of Apollo 14, he became the first man to play golf on the moon. He hit two golf balls with a makeshift club he had brought with him. In the moon's lesser gravity, the balls went further than they would have on Earth.

Astronauts of the Apollo program (1961–1972) won the race to the moon against the rival Soviet **cosmonauts**.

In little more than eight years after President Kennedy called for putting a man on the moon, Apollo 11 astronauts Neil Armstrong, Edwin "Buzz" Aldrin Jr., and Michael Collins fulfilled his vision. Armstrong and Aldrin became the first two humans to walk on the moon on July 20–21, 1969. Collins piloted the command module alone in **lunar** orbit until Armstrong and Aldrin returned. All three made it back to Earth safely.

After the Apollo program ended, NASA's space efforts focused largely on the Space Shuttle program, officially the Space Transportation System (STS) and the International Space Station (ISS). Neither involved travel to deep space.

The STS was a manned launch vehicle program that began in 1981 and ended 20 years later. It consisted of an **orbiter** launched by two reusable rocket boosters and a disposable external tank. Its purpose was to transport people and cargo between Earth and orbiting spacecraft—such as the ISS—and glide back to Earth.

The ISS is an inhabitable artificial **satellite** in low-Earth orbit. Its first component was launched in 1998 and it was completed in 2011. It

The Space Shuttle *Atlantis* undocks from the International Space Station (ISS) on May 23, 2010. This image, featuring the ISS, was photographed by a crew member aboard the *Atlantis* while the station and shuttle began separating after their undocking. The shuttle's departure ended a seven-day visit that added a new station module, replaced station batteries, and resupplied the orbiting outpost.

provides a platform for a gravity-free environment for long-term materials and life-science and medical research aimed at deep-space exploration. Sixteen nations take part in the operation and maintenance of the ISS, chiefly the United States and Russia.

Since the Space Shuttle program ended, many of its duties have been conducted by private enterprises, such as SpaceX. The U.S. Air Force's space plane, the X-37B, flies classified military missions, but it is unmanned.

A "Flexible Path" to Mars

On January 14, 2004, President George W. Bush breathed new life into the U.S. manned space program when he addressed NASA personnel at their headquarters in Washington, D.C. He offered a new Vision for Space Exploration. "Inspired by all that has come before, and guided by clear objectives, today we set a new course for America's space program," he said. "We will give NASA a new focus and vision for future exploration. We will build new ships to carry man forward into the universe, to gain a new foothold on the moon, and to prepare for new journeys to worlds beyond our own."[1]

Clearly, the president intended for Americans to go where no one has gone before. To make that possible, he called for a new spacecraft to be developed and tested by 2008. He set a target date for the new spacecraft, designated the Crew Exploration Vehicle (CEV), to conduct its first manned mission no later than 2014. "The Crew Exploration Vehicle will be capable of ferrying astronauts and scientists to the Space Station after the shuttle is retired," he continued. "But the main purpose of this spacecraft will be to carry astronauts beyond our orbit to other worlds."[2]

The Constellation Program (CxP) grew out of NASA's efforts to meet the goals of the Vision for Space Exploration. NASA renamed the CEV as the Orion CEV, after the constellation of Orion ("the Hunter"). Designers proposed three versions of the CEV. Each would

An artist's rendering of the Orion Multipurpose Crew Vehicle (Orion MPCV) set against a backdrop of future destinations for human exploration in deep space—the moon, an asteroid, and Mars. An artist's concept (inset) depicts the Orion spacecraft approaching the Earth-orbiting International Space Station (ISS).

perform a different mission. One would shuttle personnel to the STS, the second would carry cargo there, and the third would return to the moon. Additionally, the Altair Lunar Surface Access Module was designed to accompany the SEV and land astronauts on the moon.

A NASA artist's depiction of three crewmembers working around their lunar lander on the surface of the moon. NASA named the lander Altair, after a bright star in the night sky of the Northern Hemisphere. It was planned as a key component of the since-canceled Constellation Program.

To launch the Orion, the agency designed two booster rockets, the Ares I and Ares V. (Ares is the Greek equivalent of Mars, the Roman god of war.) Ares I was to be used for launching the CEV and Ares V for cargo. As the program progressed, however, it became clear that it was costing too much for available funding to cover. After a detailed review, the Constellation Program was canceled in 2010.

FAST FACT ✏️

President Bush's Vision for Space Exploration proposed much more than the creation of a new spacecraft. It also set goals for completing the International Space Station by 2010, the continued use of the Space Shuttle until then, and a return to the moon by 2020. To help meet these goals, the president called on Congress to increase NASA's budget by $1 billion over the next five years, with more to come as warranted.

Ares I is the crew launch vehicle that will carry the Orion crew exploration vehicle to space.

Ares V is the cargo launch vehicle that will deliver large-scale hardware, including the lunar lander, to space.

A conceptual image portraying a side-by-side comparison of NASA's next-generation launch vehicle systems.

That same year, President Barack Obama hosted a space conference, in which he revealed an alternate plan for moving forward in space. It was based on the findings of a presidential commission on the future of U.S. manned spaceflight. The commission was chaired by former Lockheed Martin Corporation CEO Norman Augustine. It concluded that "Mars is the ultimate destination for human exploration, but it is not the best first destination." Instead, it offered a "flexible path"[3] to explore other parts of the solar system.

The panel defined this path as a strategy under which "humans would visit sites never visited before and extend our knowledge of how to operate in space—while traveling greater and greater distances from Earth."[4] Accordingly, NASA decided to take a step-by-step approach to reaching Mars.

FAST FACT

The SLS will ultimately stand 384 feet (117 meters) tall on the launch pad. It will generate more than 9 million pounds (40 million newtons) of thrust—more than 34 times the power of a 747 jetliner.

The first focus of the Orion program would be returning to the moon. It would then move on to near-Earth asteroids, then the moons of Mars, and eventually to Mars itself. To this end, NASA opted in 2011 to develop a single, versatile crew vehicle based on the Orion CEV spacecraft designs. "We made this choice based on the progress that's been made to date," said NASA administrator Doug Cooke. "It made the most sense to stick with it [the Orion design]."[5]

NASA combined the three **variants** of the Orion CEV into a single design and renamed it the Orion Multipurpose Crew Vehicle (MPCV). Its basic design consists of two modules—the crew module and the service module. NASA contracted with Lockheed Martin to build the crew module and the European Space Agency (ESA) to develop the service module. Airbus Defense and Space will build it.

Three attachments supplement the two modules at launch. The Launch Abort Tower (LAT) attaches to the nose of the crew module. It safely removes the crew in an emergency. The service module attaches to the crew module. A Spacecraft Adapter (SA) fastens the service module to the Space Launch System core-stage rocket. Three disposable **fairings** wrap around the service module to protect it during launch.

To send the Orion spacecraft on its way to deep space, the Space Launch System is currently under development. It consists of a huge core-stage rocket and two strap-on booster rockets, derived from the Space Shuttle external tank and boosters. The SLS is a heavy expendable launch vehicle. Its core stage measures more than 130 feet (40 meters) in height and 27 feet (8 meters) in diameter. It is being built by the Boeing Corporation at NASA's Michoud Assembly Facility in Louisiana. When completed, it will represent the largest component of the SLS. Fully assembled, it will be the largest, most powerful rocket in existence. It is on track to launch the Orion spacecraft for the first time in 2019.

A conceptual image of the SLS Block 1 configuration.

4
Back in the Game

As NASA's prime contractor for the Orion Crew Exploration Vehicle (CEV), Lockheed Martin Space Systems Company leads a nationwide industrial team. Its network of major and minor subcontractors encompasses 88 facilities across the country. Another 500 small businesses throughout the nation form an expansive supply chain. Lockheed Martin maintains facilities in California, Colorado, Florida, Louisiana, and Texas to support Orion's design and development. The company also invests in a network of laboratories from Arizona to Virginia that assess risks and analyze systems, helping to reduce project costs, schedule, and risks.[1]

Subcontractors play a large role in the design, **fabrication**, and testing of many of Orion's systems and components. ATK (Alliant Techsystems Inc.) tests motors for Orion's launch abort system. Aerojet provides ongoing testing for Orion's motors and engines. United Space Alliance handcrafts all of Orion's thermal tiles. Hamilton Sundstrand's engineers develop Orion's life-support and power systems. Honeywell's engineers develop avionics and software to support data, communications, and navigation.[2]

Small businesses provide a variety of skills and engineering services essential to Orion's development, such as risk management and various analyses and studies. They also design, develop, and manufacture advanced space-flight hardware to support all of the spacecraft's systems.[3]

A weld inspector examines the bulkhead and nose cone of the Orion spacecraft. The two components are joined together using friction stir welding at NASA's Michoud Facility, New Orleans, Louisiana. The vehicle is inverted in the fixture for welding. Nondestructive techniques evaluate and validate the strength and integrity of the welds. The spacecraft is then prepped for ground testing in flight-like environments. Tests include static vibration, acoustics, and water landing. A weld technician (inset) works inside the vehicle after the bulkhead and nose cone of the Orion spacecraft are welded together.

The Orion Crew and Service Module (CSM) consists of two parts—a conical crew module and a cylindrical service module.

Lockheed Martin built the first Orion crew module at the Michoud facility. It used part of the same team that supported NASA's spaceflight programs. Using the latest manufacturing and processing techniques enhance safety features for Orion's crew and maximize structural **integrity** at minimum cost.

The crew module frame features an aluminum-lithium alloy structural design. The alloy is green-colored and extremely light. Its structural components consist of a forward **bulkhead**, an aft bulkhead and barrel, and backbone structure. It uses the latest friction stir welding (FSW) techniques. Aluminum-lithium alloy cannot be welded by traditional means.

Friction stir welding uses frictional heat to turn the metals into a plastic-like state before reaching the melting point. It then stirs them together under pressure to complete the bond. FSW produces the optimal structural integrity needed for the harsh environment of space. The module requires a total of 33 FSW welds.[4]

The Orion crew module provides habitable transportation for the crew and storage for consumables (food, drink, etc.) and research instruments. It is reusable and the only part of the

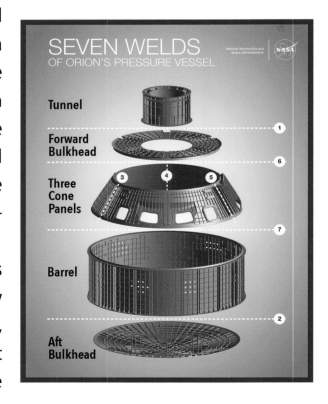

SEVEN WELDS
OF ORION'S PRESSURE VESSEL

Tunnel

Forward Bulkhead

Three Cone Panels

Barrel

Aft Bulkhead

The NASA team at its Michoud Assembly Facility completes the final weld on the first space-bound Orion capsule. It was then shipped to Kennedy Space Center for final assembly and checkout operations in preparation for Exploration Flight Test 1 (EFT-1). The Lockheed Martin team (inset) inspects the Orion crew module ground test structure prior to shipping.

MPCV that returns to Earth after each mission. Its external, 57.5-degree **frustum** shape is the same as that of the Apollo spacecraft, but the Orion crew module is larger, heavier, and equipped with advanced avionics.

The command module uses digital controls like those of the 787 Dreamliner aircraft. An auxiliary propulsion system maintains its three-axis attitude before and during reentry. Its avionics, life-support, propulsion, and thermal protection systems are designed to be upgradeable as new technology becomes available. An onboard recycling system converts waste water and urine into drinking and cooling water. An improved waste-management system features a camping-style toilet. NASA plans to use each command module for up to 10 flights.

After installing a back-shell tile panel on the Orion crew module, technicians inside the Operations and Checkout Building's high bay at NASA's Kennedy Space Center in Florida wearing clean-room suits check the fit next to the middle back shell tile panel. An artist's cutaway rendering (inset) of the crew module shows the internal layout of the equipment located between the outer shell and inner pressure vessel.

The service module is being built by Airbus Space and Defense in Bremen, Germany, for the European Space Agency. It supplies the primary power and propulsion for the spacecraft system. Its main engine, made by Aerojet, generates 7,500 pounds of thrust, 1,500 pounds more than

The European Service Module (ESM) for Orion will supply the spacecraft's power, in-space propulsion, and air and water for the crew, on behalf of the European Space Agency (ESA). Protective fairings, added to Orion's Service Module at the Operations and Checkout facility at Kennedy Space Center, are jettisoned above the atmosphere. The inset shows the structural test article of the ESM.

CREW MODULE

CREW MODULE ADAPTOR

EUROPEAN SERVICE MODULE

SPACECRAFT ADAPTOR JETTISONED PANELS

CREW AND SERVICE MODULE

SERVICE MODULE

SPACECRAFT ADAPTOR

NASA's first completed Orion Crew Module moves closer to its rendezvous with space. Here it sits atop its service module at the Neil Armstrong Operations and Checkout Facility at Kennedy Space Center in Florida. From there, it will transfer to another facility for fueling and then move again for installation of its Launch Abort System (LAS). Finally, complete and ready for launch, it will stack on top of the Delta IV Heavy rocket.

FAST FACT ✐

Multipurpose Crew Vehicle Specifications[5]
Builder: Lockheed Martin/European Space Agency
First crewed flight: 2021 (or later)
Launch vehicle: Space Launch System
Crew: 2 to 6
Length overall: 26 feet (8 meters)
Diameter: 16.5 feet (5 meters)
Habitable volume: 316 cubic feet (9 cubic meters)

that used on the Space Shuttle. The SM draws additional power from an "X-wing" solar array that gives it a windmill-like appearance.

Like the command module, the service module is constructed of aluminum-lithium alloy to limit weight. It consists of several building blocks—an upper cylinder, a tank platform, a main cylinder, a lower platform, an equipment deck, and a protection system to defend against space debris. A system of longerons and radial webs reinforces the service module and connects it to the command module. It is 15 feet, 8 inches (4.78 meters) long, 16 feet, 6 inches (5.03 meters) in diameter, and weighs 8,000 pounds (3,700 kilograms) when empty.[6]

The service module supports the crew module from launch through separation at reentry. When mated to the CM, its propulsion system enables orbital transfers (changes of orbits), altitude control, and aborted flights at high altitudes. It generates and stores electrical power while orbiting, and maintains the temperature of the vehicle's systems and components. It also furnishes the water and oxygen needed for a habitable environment. In every sense of the word, it is a *service* module.

Together, Orion's two main modules will provide the United States with access to deep space for the first time in almost a half-century. In the competitive environment of outer space, NASA and its astronauts are back in the game.

5
Challenges Ahead

On July 29, 1958, President Dwight D. Eisenhower signed the National Aeronautics and Space Act into law and NASA was born. Over its six-decade-long history, NASA has spearheaded space exploration. Its achievements are grand and many. Perhaps most notably, it put men on the moon and returned them safely to Earth. Americans and their friends around the world rejoiced at Neal Armstrong's "giant leap for mankind."

During the ensuing years, NASA also experienced great tragedy. Three astronauts died in the 1967 Apollo fire. The breakup of the *Challenger* space shuttle claimed seven lives in 1986. And the failed *Columbia* reentry took seven more lives in 2003. The cost of grand achievement often comes high.

Seventeen brave astronauts have paid the ultimate price for challenging the limits of earthbound humanity. Because of them, and others like them, some day humans may slip the bounds of Earth and dwell among the stars. But many challenges remain to be met and overcome on America's path to other planets.

After the *Columbia* disaster, NASA grounded the Space Shuttle program until July, 2005. *Columbia* had flown the program's first flight in 1981. The orbiter *Atlantis* ended the program with its last flight in July 2011. In all, there were 135 Space Shuttle missions. Since that time, NASA's manned spaceflight capability has been on hold.

The *Challenger*, assigned to the Space Transportation System 6 (STS-6) mission, is shown lifting off from Pad 39A at Kennedy Space Center. It carried astronauts Paul J. Weitz, Koral J. Bobko, Donald H. Peterson, and Dr. Story Musgrave. The ill-fated orbiter claimed the lives of seven astronauts (inset) on its next mission, STS-7: In the back row, from left to right, Ellison S. Onizuka, Sharon Christa McAuliffe, Greg Jarvis, and Judy Resnik. In the front row, from left to right, Michael J. Smith, Dick Scobee, and Ron McNair.

FAST FACT ✎

On January 28, 1986, on an unusually cold morning, the space shuttle orbiter *Challenger* broke apart in a twisting plume of smoke and fire, 73 seconds after it lifted off from Kennedy Space Center. An O-ring seal on *Challenger*'s solid rocket booster had become brittle in the cold temperatures and failed. Flames escaped from the booster, damaging the external fuel tank and causing the orbiter to disintegrate.

Today, NASA stands on the threshold of reclaiming its former superiority in space with the Orion program. But it is moving ahead with all due diligence, emphasizing astronaut safety. NASA incorporated the lessons learned from the *Columbia* accident into every succeeding flight. Many of Orion's safety improvements spring directly from that ill-fated flight.

4

"We're hoping nothing ever goes wrong, but if it does, we've taken every possible step to keep the crew safe and give them every possible fighting chance they can have," said Dustin Gohmert, leader of NASA's survival engineering team. "It's especially important to us that were here during the *Columbia* accident, because they were our friends, too."[1]

The *Columbia* investigation uncovered numerous flaws in the design of the orbiter's crew cabin.

FAST FACT

Shortly after launch on January 16, 2003, a piece of foam insulation broke off from *Columbia*'s propellant tank and damaged the edge of the shuttle's left wing. Upon reentry two weeks later, wind and heat entered the wing where heat-resistant tiles were damaged or missing, blowing it apart over southeast Texas.

They included defects in the seats, seatbelts, spacesuits, and life support systems. Engineers redesigned the seats for Orion based on the form-fitting seats used in professional race cars. The new seats support every part of the body and offer extreme cushioning and shock absorption in a crash. Taking inspiration from widely adjustable seatbelts in children's car seats, they designed new seatbelts to fit a broad range of crew members. The new belts provide an exact fit for all, from small females to large males.

The *Columbia* disaster revealed that the astronauts did not have time to **configure** their spacesuits against the rapidly occurring loss of pressure. Events happened so fast that some were caught without their helmets or gloves. NASA engineers gave the suits a complete makeover. The suits now inflate immediately by themselves to protect against pressure losses. And an upgraded life-support system provides a constant flow of oxygen in the capsule.

To protect crew members from the dangerous effects of radiation in space, the Orion uses the mass of equipment already onboard in the aft bay to shield them. This protects the crew while helping to keep the vehicle's weight down.

The Launch Abort System (LAS) ranks high on Orion's design innovations. It forms a part of the Launch Escape Tower (LET) that sits atop the Orion stack-up and the Space Launch System rocket. The LAS consists of six components. From the top down, they comprise a nose segment, an attitude control monitor, a forward interstage, a **jettison** motor, an abort motor, and a fairing assembly. The stack-up stands about 44 feet (13.4 meters) tall. When loaded, it weighs nearly six tons.

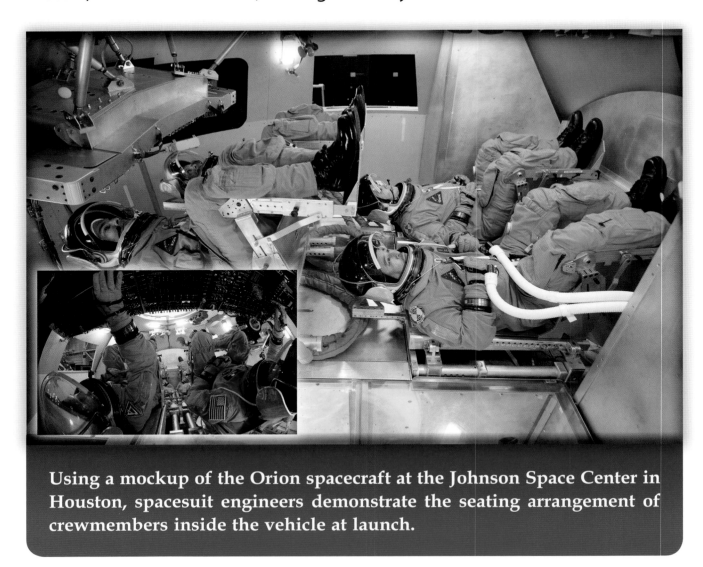

Using a mockup of the Orion spacecraft at the Johnson Space Center in Houston, spacesuit engineers demonstrate the seating arrangement of crewmembers inside the vehicle at launch.

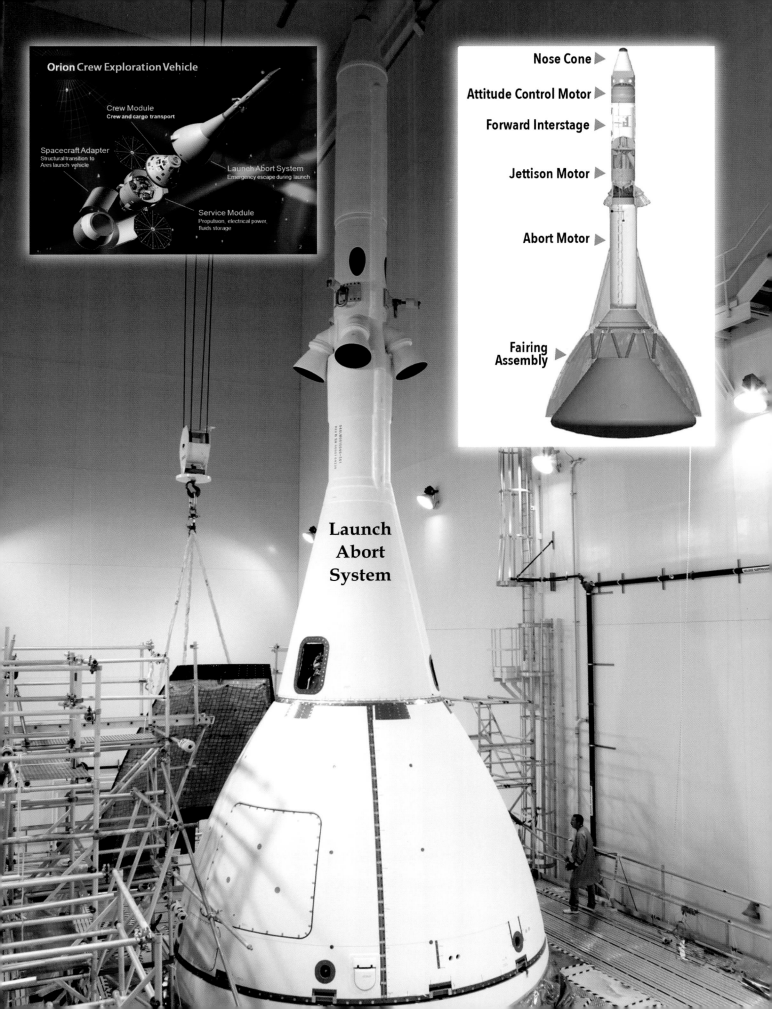

Orion Crew Exploration Vehicle

Crew Module
Crew and cargo transport

Spacecraft Adapter
Structural transition to
Ares launch vehicle

Launch Abort System
Emergency escape during launch

Service Module
Propulsion, electrical power,
fluids storage

Launch
Abort
System

Nose Cone ▶

Attitude Control Motor ▶

Forward Interstage ▶

Jettison Motor ▶

Abort Motor ▶

Fairing
Assembly ▶

In the event of an emergency during launch and later ascent stages, the LAS separates Orion's crew module from the SLS rocket. Then it uses its own propulsion system to insert the module into a lower-than-planned orbit or return it to Earth for an **impromptu** landing. This important safety feature was not available in NASA's earlier space programs.

"We're doing a whole lot of things to make [Orion] safer," Gohmert added, "and everything we've learned from the shuttle accidents, from Russian space accidents, automobile accidents—we've taken lessons from all of them and tried to incorporate them into Orion."[2] In so doing, NASA and its space partners have created an engineering masterwork.

An artist's concept of Orion's Launch Abort System's Attitude Control Motor (ACM) in operation during an aborted mission. Orbital ATK collaborated with NASA and Lockheed Martin to complete a recent test of the ACM.

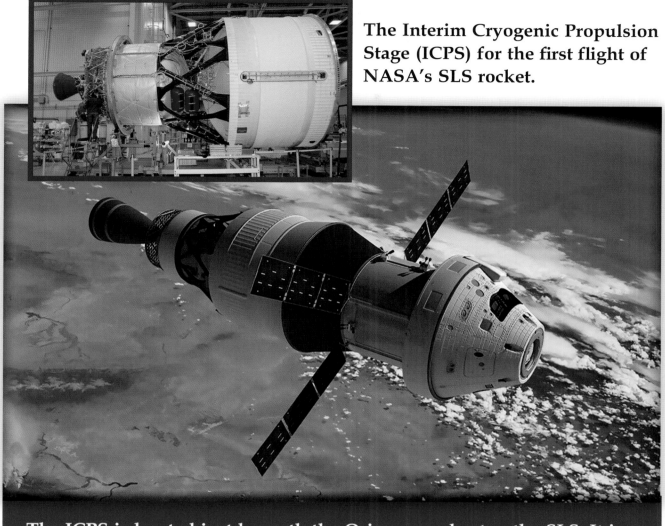

The Interim Cryogenic Propulsion Stage (ICPS) for the first flight of NASA's SLS rocket.

The ICPS is located just beneath the Orion capsule atop the SLS. It is a liquid oxygen/liquid hydrogen-based system. On Exploration Mission 1 (EM-1), the first test mission of the Orion and the SLS together, it will provide the power needed to push Orion beyond the moon before it returns to Earth. The exploratory vehicle is designed to carry its crew to space, provide emergency abort capability, sustain the crew during space travel, and enable safe reentry from deep-space return velocities.

Orion—America's next generation spacecraft—is superbly equipped to meet and overcome whatever challenges that might lie ahead on the way to Mars. In 2019, it is scheduled to mate with the Space Launch System for the first time. In an unmanned flight designated Exploration Mission 1, Orion will take the next step.

WHAT YOU SHOULD KNOW

☆ A single launch of the Space Launch System costs about $500 million.

☆ The cost of the total Orion program is estimated at more than $20 billion.

☆ Orion's largest setback occurred when engineers discovered cracks in three adjacent radial ribs of the spacecraft after high-pressure testing in November 2012. The cracks were repaired without having to remanufacture the vehicle.

☆ Habitable volume in the Orion spacecraft is 30 percent larger than Apollo.

☆ Similar but different back-up systems prevent the risk of single-point failures.

☆ Automated functions such as guidance and navigation systems free astronauts to perform other tasks.

☆ Orion's life-support system recycles air, and clears heat, moisture, and odors generated during physical activity, allowing astronauts to exercise. It also recognizes hazardous situations and recovers from them.

☆ The spacecraft structure is designed to withstand micrometeoroid (small meteor) strikes.

☆ Onboard computer systems and software can withstand exposure to intense radiation.

☆ Orion's launch abort system can activate within **milliseconds** to pull its crew to safety and position the module for a safe landing. Its motor generates enough thrust to lift 26 elephants off the ground.

☆ On Orion's projected trip to Mars, the plan calls for it to launch from Earth and then dock with a larger habitat module in space before beginning its long journey.

QUICK STATS

✶ Orion's advanced avionics and life-saving safety systems require more than 20 miles of cabling, wire harnesses, and tubing.

✶ Computers running software on Orion can process 480 million instructions per second.

✶ A successful launch requires thousands of steps to be carried out in precise order and often at the same time.

✶ Orion's launch abort system protects crew members during ascent but must be jettisoned within 6 minutes and 20 seconds of launch, because it blocks the parachutes that allow the spacecraft to splash down safely.

✶ The launch abort system is just the first of 17 separations or jettisons that must occur exactly as planned for the operation to be successful.

✶ The STS rocket stands taller than the Statue of Liberty and generates more than 8.4 million pounds (3.8 million kilograms) of thrust, equal to 135 jet engines used on the Boeing 747 jetliner.

✶ The chance of an onboard computer going down is estimated at one in every 3.7 missions and a one-in-8,500 chance for a second computer. Orion carries a third computer. The chance of losing all three computers at the same time is one in 1,870,000 missions.

✶ Orion's 3-screen cockpit design replaces 2,000 switches and controls used in the Space Shuttle.

1958 James A. Van Allen discovers radiation belts in Earth's magnetic field. NASA is born.

1961 Alan Shepard becomes the first American in space. President John F. Kennedy calls for America's space program to put a man on the moon by the end of the decade.

1962 John Glenn Jr. becomes the first American to orbit the Earth.

1969 Neil Armstrong and Edwin "Buzz" Aldrin Jr. become the first two humans to walk on the moon on July 20-21, 1969.

1971 Alan Shepard hits two golf balls on the moon.

1981 Space Transportation System (Space Shuttle) missions begin; they end in 2011.

1986 The *Challenger* disaster claims seven lives.

1998 Construction begins on the International Space Station; it ends in 2011.

2004 President George W. Bush offers a new Vision for Space Exploration and calls for a new spacecraft to be developed and tested by 2008. The Constellation Program grows out of NASA's efforts to meet the goals of President Bush but is canceled in 2010.

2005 The *Columbia* breaks up and seven astronauts die.

2011 NASA opts to develop a single, versatile crew vehicle based on the Orion CEV spacecraft designs.

2014 Orion successfully completes its first uncrewed test flight, Exploration Flight Test 1 (EFT-1).

2019 Space Launch System (SLS) is scheduled to launch the unmanned Orion spacecraft for the first time, though the actual launch date may slip to 2020 or later.

2021 The first manned flight of the Orion spacecraft is scheduled; it may be postponed until 2023 or later.

Chapter 1—Back to the Future

1. Nola Taylor Redd, "How Long Does It Take to Get to Mars?" Space. com. February 13, 2014. http://www.space.com/24701-how-long-does-it-take-to-get-to-mars.html

2. Andrew Chaikin and the editors of Time-Life Books, *A Man on the Moon: One Giant Leap*. Vol. 1. (Richmond, VA: Time-Life Books, 1999), p. 311.

3. Christopher A. Veloicaza, "USS Anchorage Departs on NASA's Orion Mission." America's Navy. December 2, 2014. http://www.public.navy.mil/surfor/lpd23/Pages/uss-anchorage-departs-on-nasa-s-orion-mission.aspx#.WS3ejca1uM8

4. "NASA's New Orion Spacecraft Completes First Spaceflight Test." NASA. December 4, 2014. https://www.nasa.gov/press/2014/december/nasa-s-new-orion-spacecraft-completes-first-spaceflight-test

5. Ibid.

6. Alan Boyle, "Orion Test Flight Brings Back That Old Apollo Feeling at NASA." NBC News. December 3, 2014. http://www.nbcnews.com/science/space/orion-test-flight-brings-back-old-apollo-feeling-nasa-n260856

Chapter 2—New Life

1. Ellie Zolfagharifard et al., "The view from space at 20,000 mph and 4000°F." dailymail.com. December 5, 2014. http://www.dailymail.co.uk/sciencetech/article-2862440/Splashdown-Orion-successfully-lands-Pacific-Ocean-two-historic-orbits-Earth.html

2. Ibid.

3. "Apollo 11 Moon Landing." John F. Kennedy Presidential Library and Museum. https://www.jfklibrary.org/JFK/JFK-Legacy/Apollo_11_Moon_Landing.aspx

Chapter 3—A Flexible Path to Mars

1. "President Bush Announces New Vision for Space Exploration Program." NASA. January 2004. https://history.nasa.gov/Bush%20SEP.htm

2. Ibid.

3. George Leopold, "Augustine panel urges 'flexible path' to Mars." *EETimes*. September 8, 2009. http://www.eetimes.com/document.asp?doc_id=1171651

4. Ibid.

5. Elizabeth Howell, "Lockheed Martin: Prime Contractor for Orion Spacecraft." space.com. March 24, 2016. http://www.space.com/19528-lockheed-martin.html

Chapter 4—Back in the Game

1. *Orion: America's Next Generation Spacecraft* (National Aeronautics and Space Administration. eBook. Washington, D.C.: Progressive Management, 2012), Kindle Locations 89–97.

2. Ibid., Kindle Locations 97–104.

3. Ibid., Kindle Locations 105–107.

4. Ibid., Kindle Locations 189–196.

5. Karl Tate, "Orion Explained: NASA's Multi-Purpose Crew Vehicle (Infographic)." space.com. January 16, 2013. http://space.com/19292-nasa-orion-space-capsule-explained-infographic.html

6. "Orion (spacecraft)." Space Wiki. http://space.wikia.com/wiki/Orion_(spacecraft)

Chapter 5—Challenges Ahead

1. Clara Moskowitz, "How the Columbia Shuttle Disaster Changed Spacecraft Safety Forever." space.com. January 29, 2013. http://www.space.com/19509-columbia-shuttle-disaster-spacecraft-safety.html

2. Ibid.

Aguilar, David A. *Space Encyclopedia: A Tour of Our Solar System and Beyond*. Washington, D.C.: National Geographic Kids, 2013.

Anderson, Amy, and Brian Anderson. *Space Dictionary for Kids: The Everything Guide for Kids Who Love Space*. Waco, TX: Prufrock Press, 2016.

Earl, C. F. *Private Space Exploration*. Kid's Library of Space Exploration Series. Vestal, NY: Village Earth Press, 2016.

Etingoff, Kim. *Missions to Mars*. Kid's Library of Space Exploration Series. Vestal, NY: Village Earth Press, 2016.

Jones, Tom. *Ask the Astronaut: A Galaxy of Astonishing Answers to Your Questions on Spaceflight*. Washington, D.C.: Smithsonian Books, 2016.

WORKS CONSULTED

"Apollo 11 Moon Landing." John F. Kennedy Presidential Library and Museum. https://www.jfklibrary.org/JFK/JFK-Legacy/Apollo_11_Moon_Landing.aspx

Boyle, Alan. "Orion Test Flight Brings Back That Old Apollo Feeling at NASA." NBC News. December 3, 2014. http://www.nbcnews.com/science/space/orion-test-flight-brings-back-old-apollo-feeling-nasa-n260856

Chaikin, Andrew and the editors of Time-Life Books. *A Man on the Moon: One Giant Leap*. Vol. 1. Richmond, VA: Time-Life Books, 1999.

Howell, Elizabeth. "Lockheed Martin: Prime Contractor for Orion Spacecraft." space.com. March 24, 2016. http://www.space.com/19528-lockheed-martin.html

Leopold, George. "Augustine panel urges 'flexible path' to Mars." *EETimes*. September 8, 2009. http://www.eetimes.com/document.asp?doc_id=1171651

Moskowitz, Clara. "How the Columbia Shuttle Disaster Changed Spacecraft Safety Forever." space.com. January 29, 2013. http://www.space.com/19509-columbia-shuttle-disaster-spacecraft-safety.html

"NASA's New Orion Spacecraft Completes First Spaceflight Test." NASA. December 4, 2014. https://www.nasa.gov/press/2014/december/nasa-s-new-orion-spacecraft-completes-first-spaceflight-test

Orion: America's Next Generation Spacecraft. National Aeronautics and Space Administration. eBook. Washington, D.C.: Progressive Management, 2012.

"Orion (spacecraft)." Space Wiki. http://space.wikia.com/wiki/Orion_(spacecraft)

"President Bush Announces New Vision for Space Exploration Program." NASA. January 2004. https://history.nasa.gov/Bush%20SEP.htm

Redd, Nola Taylor. "How Long Does It Take to Get to Mars?" space.com. February 13, 2014. http://www.space.com/24701-how-long-does-it-take-to-get-to-mars.html

Tate, Karl. "Orion Explained: NASA's Multi-Purpose Crew Vehicle (Infographic)." SPACE.com. January 16, 2013. http://space.com/19292-nasa-orion-space-capsule-explained-infographic.html

Veloicaza, Christopher A. "USS Anchorage Departs on NASA's Orion Mission." America's Navy. December 2, 2014. http://www.public.navy.mil/surfor/lpd23/Pages/uss-anchorage-departs-on-nasa-sorion-mission.aspx#.WS3ejca1uM8

Zolfagharifard, Ellie, et al. "The view from space at 20,000mph and 4000°F." dailymail.com. December 5, 2014. http://www.dailymail.co.uk/sciencetech/article-2862440/Splashdown-Orion-successfully-lands-Pacific-Ocean-two-historic-orbits-Earth.html

ON THE INTERNET

Orion Activities and Coloring Sheets for Kids. NASA. https://www.nasa.gov/centers/johnson/about/resources/jscfacts/activity_coloring_sheets.html

Orion (spacecraft). KidzSearch. http://wiki.kidzsearch.com/wiki/Orion_(spacecraft)

"What Is Orion?" NASA. March 25, 2015. https://www.nasa.gov/audience/forstudents/k-4/stories/nasa-knows/what-is-orion-k4.html

astronaut (AS-troh-nawt)—a person trained to travel in a spacecraft

Avcoat (AV-coat)—an epoxy resin with special additives in a fiberglass honeycomb matrix; developed by Avco and used as a heat shield

bulkhead (BULK-hed)—an upright partition in a ship, aircraft, or vehicle

configure (kohn-FIG-yure)—to arrange, shape, or outline

cosmonaut (KOZ-moh-nawt)—an astronaut, especially one from Russia or the former Soviet Union

deep space—the regions beyond the gravitational pull of the Earth

déjà vu (DAY-zhah VOO)—a feeling that one has seen or heard something before

fabrication (fab-ri-KAY-shun)—act of constructing or manufacturing

fairings (FARE-ingz)— external structures that increase streamlining and reduce drag

frustum (FRUS-tuhm)—the remainder of a cone or pyramid whose upper part has been cut off by a plane parallel to the base

impromptu (im-PROMP-too)—without preparation or rehearsal

integration (in-teh-GRAY-shun)—the act of bringing together smaller components into a single system

integrity (in-TEG-ri-tee)—soundness; an unimpaired condition

jettison (JET-i-sohn)—to throw something overboard, especially from a ship in distress to lighten it

lunar (LOO-nahr)—of or derived from the moon

millisecond (MIL-i-sek-ohnd)—one-thousandth of a second

module (MAW-jool)—an independently-operable unit that is part of the total structure of a space vehicle or system

newtons (NOO-tuhnz)—units of force named for Sir Isaac Newton

orbiter (OR-bi-tehr)—a spacecraft or artificial satellite in orbit or designed to be in orbit

retrograde (RET-roh-grayd)—moving backward; having or being motion in a direction contrary to that of the general motion of similar bodies and especially east to west among the stars

satellite (SAT-eh-lyte)—a heavenly body revolving around a planet; an artificial body placed in orbit

solar (SOH-lahr)—of or derived from the sun

variant (VAIR-ee-ahnt)—differing from something or a standard

ABOUT THE AUTHOR

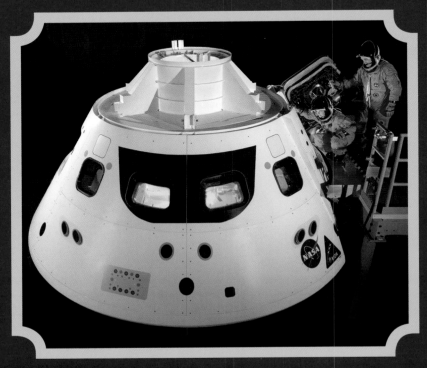

Earle Rice Jr. is a former senior design engineer and technical writer in the aerospace, electronic-defense, and nuclear industries. He has devoted full time to his writing since 1993. In the 1980s, he served as a senior field engineer and procedures engineer on the Space Shuttle Program at Vandenberg Air Force Base, California. Earle is the author of more than ninety published books. He is listed in *Who's Who in America* and is a member of the Society of Children's Book Writers and Illustrators, the League of World War I Aviation Historians, the Air Force Association, and the Disabled American Veterans.